CONTEMPORARY AMERICAN SUCCESS STORIES

Famous People of Hispanic Heritage

Volume VIII

Valerie Menard
Melanie Cole

A Mitchell Lane
Multicultural Biography Series
• Celebrating Diversity •

CONTEMPORARY AMERICAN SUCCESS STORIES
Famous People of Hispanic Heritage

VOLUME I
Geraldo Rivera
Melissa Gonzalez
Federico Peña
Ellen Ochoa

VOLUME II
Tommy Nuñez
Margarita Esquiroz
Cesar Chavez
Antonia Novello

VOLUME III
Giselle Fernandez
Jon Secada
Desi Arnaz
Joan Baez

VOLUME IV
Selena Quintanilla Pérez
Robert Rodriguez
Josefina López
Alfredo Estrada

VOLUME V
Gloria Estefan
Fernando Cuza
Rosie Perez
Cheech Marin

VOLUME VI
Pedro José Greer
Nancy Lopez
Rafael Palmeiro
Hilda Perera

VOLUME VII
Mary Joe Fernandez
Raul Julia
Mariah Carey
Andres Galarraga

VOLUME VIII
Cristina Saralegui
Trent Dimas
Nydia Velázquez
Jimmy Smits

VOLUME IX
Roy Benavidez
Isabel Allende
Oscar De La Hoya
Jackie Guerra

Publisher's Cataloging in Publication
Menard, Valerie, and Melanie Cole.
    Famous people of Hispanic heritage. Vol. VIII / Valerie Menard and
Melanie Cole.
    p. cm. —(Contemporary American success stories)—(A Mitchell Lane
multicultural biography series)
    Includes index.
    LCCN: 95-75963
    ISBN: 1-883845-42-4 (hc)
    ISBN: 1-883845-41-6 (pbk)

    1. Hispanic Americans—Biography—Juvenile literature. I. Title.
II. Series.

E184.S75M37   1997   920'.009268
                            QBI96-20404

Illustrated by Barbara Tidman
Project Editor: Susan R. Scarfe

Mitchell Lane
PUBLISHERS
Your Path To Quality Educational Material

P.O. Box 200
Childs, Maryland 21916-0200

TABLE OF CONTENTS

Acknowledgments

Every reasonable effort has been made to gain copyright permission where such permission has been deemed necessary. Any oversight brought to the publisher's attention will be corrected in future printings.

Most of the stories in this series were written through personal interviews and/or with the complete permission of the person, representative of the person, or family of the person being profiled and are authorized biographies. Though we attempted to contact each and every person profiled within, for various reasons we were unable to authorize every story. All stories have been thoroughly researched and checked for accuracy, and to the best of our knowledge represent true stories.

We wish to acknowledge with gratitude the generous help of Cristina Saralegui (telephone interview November 6, 1996) and her generosity for supplying us with photographs; Trent Dimas (telephone interview August 1996 and others) and Lisa Dimas for help with our story about Trent and for allowing us use of their personal photos; and Nydia Velázquez (telephone interview December 10, 1996) for her patience and help with photographs and our story of her.

Photograph Credits

The quality of the photographs in this book may vary; many of them are personal snapshots supplied to us courtesy of the person being profiled. Many are very old, one-of-a-kind photos. Most are not professional photographs, nor were they intended to be. The publisher felt that the personal nature of the stories in this book would only be enhanced by real-life, family album–type photos, and chose to include many interesting snapshots, even if they were not quite the best quality. pp. 8, 30, 54, 76 sketches by Barbara Tidman; pp. 11, 12, 13, 14, 16, 19, 23, 25, 29 courtesy Cristina Saralegui; pp. 32, 33, 34, 35, 36, 38, 45, 47, 48, 52, 53 courtesy Trent and Lisa Dimas; p. 43 AP Photo; p. 44 Reuters/Michael Probst/Archive Photos; p. 68 AP Photo/Ed Bailey; p. 69 Andrea Renault, Globe Photos; pp. 71, 73, 74 courtesy Nydia Velázquez; p. 81 Fitzroy Barrett, Globe Photos; p. 84 UPI/Corbis-Bettmann; p. 85 courtesy Fox Film Corporation; p. 86 Globe Photos; p. 88 courtesy Cinema Plus L.P.; p. 89 courtesy Columbia Pictures; p. 91 courtesy New Line Cinema; p. 92 Fitzroy Barrett, Globe Photos; p. 93 AP Photo.

About the Authors

Valerie Menard has been an editor for *Hispanic* magazine since the magazine moved to Austin, Texas, in July 1994. Before joining the magazine, she was a managing editor of a bilingual weekly, *La Prensa*. Valerie writes from a Latino perspective and as an advocate for Latino causes.

Melanie Cole has been a writer and editor for seventeen years. She was previously an associate editor of *Texas Monthly* and is now managing editor of *Hispanic* magazine. She has published numerous poems, articles, and reviews in various journals, magazines, and newspapers. A native of Kansas, Ms. Cole now resides in Austin, Texas.

INTRODUCTION

by Kathy Escamilla

One of the fastest growing ethno-linguistic groups in the United States is a group of people who are collectively called Hispanic. The term *Hispanic* is an umbrella term that encompasses people from many nationalities, from all races, and from many social and cultural groups. The label *Hispanic* sometimes obscures the diversity of people who come from different countries and speak different varieties of Spanish. Therefore, it is crucial to know that the term *Hispanic* encompasses persons whose origins are from Spanish-speaking countries, including Spain, Mexico, Central and South America, Cuba, Puerto Rico, the Dominican Republic, and the United States. It is important also to note that Spanish is the heritage language of most Hispanics. However, Hispanics living in the United States are also linguistically diverse. Some speak mostly Spanish and little English, others are bilingual, and some speak only English.

Hispanics are often also collectively called Latinos. In addition to calling themselves Hispanics or Latinos, many people in this group also identify themselves in more specific terms according to their country of origin or their ethnic group (e.g., Cuban-American, Chicano, Puerto Rican-American, etc.). The population of Hispanics in the United States is expected to triple in the next twenty-five years, making it imperative that students in schools understand and appreciate the enormous contributions that persons of Hispanic heritage have made in the Western Hemisphere in general and in the United States in particular.

There are many who believe that in order to be successful in the United States now and in the twenty-first century, all persons from diverse cultural backgrounds, such as Hispanics, should be assimilated. To be assimilated means losing one's distinct cultural and linguistic heritage and changing to or adopting the cultural attributes of the dominant culture.

Others disagree with the assimilationist viewpoint and believe that it is both possible and desirable for persons from diverse cultural backgrounds to maintain their cultural heritage and also to contribute positively and successfully to the dominant culture. This viewpoint is called cultural pluralism, and it is from the perspective of cultural pluralism that these biographies are written. They represent persons who identify strongly with their Hispanic heritage and at the same time who are proud of being citizens of the United States and successful contributors to U.S. society.

The biographies in these books represent the diversity of Hispanic heritage in the United States. Persons featured are contemporary figures whose national origins range from Argentina to Arizona and whose careers and contributions cover many aspects of contemporary life in the United States. These biographies include writers, musicians, actors, journalists, astronauts, businesspeople, judges, political activists, and politicians. Further, they include Hispanic women and men, and thus also characterize the changing role of all women in the United States. Each person profiled in this book is a positive role model, not only for persons of Hispanic heritage, but for any person.

Collectively, these biographies demonstrate the value of cultural pluralism and a view that the future strength of the United States lies in nurturing the diversity of its human potential, not in its uniformity.

Dr. Kathy Escamilla is currently Vice President of the National Association for Bilingual Education and an Associate Professor of Bilingual Education and Multicultural Education at the University of Colorado, Denver. She previously taught at the University of Arizona, and was the Director of Bilingual Education for the Tucson Unified School District in Tucson, Arizona. Dr. Escamilla earned a B.A. degree in Spanish and Literature from the University of Colorado in 1971. Her master's degree is in bilingual education from the University of Kansas, and she earned her doctorate in bilingual education from UCLA in 1987.

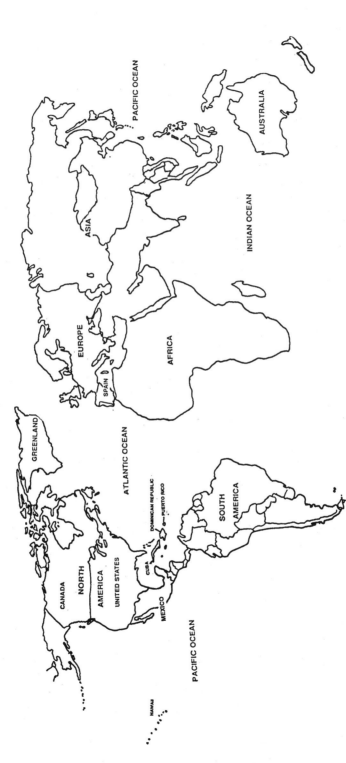

MAP OF THE WORLD

CRISTINA SARALEGUI

Journalist, Talk Show Host
1948–

"Pay attention when living your life. Time is the most valuable asset we have, and so often we just throw it away. Enjoy life. Live with passion and dream big. Don't be afraid to dream and set goals to make those big dreams come true.**"**

Cristina Saralegui, as told to Valerie Menard, November 1996

BIO HIGHLIGHTS

- Born January 29, 1948, Havana, Cuba; mother: Cristina Santamarina; father: Francisco Saralegui
- 1960, left Cuba in exile, moved to Florida and began keeping a journal
- Attended the University of Miami to study journalism
- Received internship at *Vanidades* magazine
- 1979, named editor in chief of *Cosmopolitan en Español*
- Married Marcos Avila, June 9, 1984
- 1989, became executive producer of *El Show de Cristina*; six months later, show rated number one in its time slot
- 1990, *El Show de Cristina* won an Emmy Award
- December 1995, honored by the American Foundation for AIDS Research (AmFar) with an award for Distinction for Leadership in Communications and Broadcasting

Francisco told his family to pack for a trip, that they were leaving Havana that night.

The year was 1960, and it seemed like a normal night in Havana, Cuba. But as Francisco Saralegui gathered his family, twelve-year-old Cristina, Francisco's oldest child, knew it would change her life forever. Francisco told his family to pack for a trip, that they were leaving Havana that night. Though her four siblings—Victoria, Francisco Jr., Maria, and Ignacio—assumed the family was going on vacation, Cristina took a moment during all the fuss to walk outside, look at the moon out over the sea, and memorize every sight and smell of her home. "My father only told us we were leaving, not that we were leaving forever," remembers Cristina. "But somehow I knew and I made a point of remembering everything I could to take with me." She showed insight then, but even a frightened little girl could never dream that she would one day be the host of the most popular, Emmy Award-winning, Spanish-language talk show on television, *El Show de Cristina.*

Cristina Saralegui did indeed become one of the most popular talk show hosts in the U.S. and Latin America as the star and creator of *El Show de Cristina*, which is broadcast on the Univision television network. It is televised in over eighteen countries in Latin America as well as in the U.S., and it has a viewing audience of 100 million. But that scary last night in Havana has never left Cristina's memory. "Thirty-seven years later, I still feel the sorrow that loomed over me that day, because I knew I was not coming back, ever, or at least for a very long time," she says. "That feeling holds true to this day."

The Saralegui family had established a publishing empire in Latin America. They owned three magazines, including *Vanidades*, a Spanish-language fashion magazine and the only one they brought with them to the U.S. Both her father and mother, Cristina Santamarina, were born in Havana. Her grandfather on her mother's side, José, was a prominent advertising man in Cuba and was responsible for many of the most successful advertising campaigns during the 1950s. Her grandfather on her father's side, Francisco, was an executive at the Reciprocity Trading Company in Cuba, which imported, among other goods, all of the paper

Cristina, as a baby, with her mother and father. Taken in Cuba, 1948

that was used on the island. The family's connection to paper led them into the magazine business.

Cristina is two years old in this portrait.

Her mother, says Cristina, had been raised to be a housewife, but she rebelled against her parents' intentions and instead went to work for Pan American Airlines after graduating from high school. She quit work only after marrying Cristina's father, whom she had met at a softball game. "My mom was playing for her high school team in Havana. My dad fell head over heals for her and started courting her—without luck at first—until she gave in." Francisco studied engineering in school but opted to follow his natural instincts as an entrepreneur.

CRISTINA SARALEGUI

Cristina, or Mati, as she's called, was born on January 29, 1948. Her sister Victoria was born two years later; Francisco Jr., in 1952; Maria, in 1956; and Ignacio, in 1962. She received her nickname from one of her brothers, who couldn't pronounce *Cristina* and instead called her Matitina, which was eventually shortened to Mati.

Cristina (right) with her mother and sister Victoria

Before the revolution, Cristina says her life was like the lives of most kids her age, though maybe a little more strict. She attended a Catholic convent school for girls, and even its name reveals that it wasn't your average elementary school. It was called *Esclavas del Corazón Sagrado* (Slaves of the Sacred Heart) and was run by an order of nuns with the same name. "We used to laugh that although the nuns were supposed to be the slaves, in reality we [the students] were," jokes Cristina. But things weren't all bad.

CRISTINA SARALEGUI

Her education in Cuba, she feels, was excellent and prepared her for life in the United States. She became friends with Mrs. Rogers, a woman who had taught her since the first grade. She was her English teacher. Mrs. Rogers had a

daughter about Cristina's age. She would invite Cristina to her house to play with her little girl, and it was during this time that Cristina remembers she really learned to speak fluent English. "Mrs. Rogers loved me. I spoke perfect English thanks to Mrs. Rogers and all the Hop-Along Cassidy movies I saw at her house." Cristina was happy growing up in Cuba.

But in 1959, everything changed. Fidel Castro led a communist revolution that affected the lives of many Cuban families, including the Saraleguis. After Castro assumed control of the country, he eliminated private ownership. All property was to be owned by "the people," which really meant the government. A wealthy Cuban family like the Saraleguis were a quick target for the new communist government, and once the family's property was taken by it, Francisco Saralegui knew that it was only a matter of time before he and his family might be jailed or executed in the name of the revolution.

Cristina at nine years old, taken in Cuba

"The telephone companies had already been taken by the government," says Cristina, and for this reason, her father waited until the last minute to prepare the family. "He knew he couldn't tell us in advance because we might tell someone. We couldn't say good-bye to anyone. I had a boyfriend and I couldn't say good-bye to him. My father couldn't take any chance that the government would find out and be waiting for us at the airport and not allow us to leave."

Once the revolution broke out, Cristina's normal childhood came to an end. No place in Cuba was safe during that time. Cristina says that it was not unusual to hear of bombings, and one of the regular bombing targets was movie theaters. "You couldn't even go to the movies for fear of a bombing," she says. She also remembers how people began to grow used to the sound of shootings, which would break out at any time. "I remember being in a geography class and hearing the pa-pa-pa-pa-pomp of a gun and the teacher shouting, 'Everybody hit the floor,' and we would. As soon as it was over, we would just start class again. By the end of that year there were just three or four of us in that class, because either the parents were terrified and would not send the kids to school or everybody had left already for exile, to Spain, Miami or Mexico."

Although the family did arrive safely in the United States, getting used to life here would take a few years. As Cristina puts it, "We came

▼▼▼▼▼
"My father couldn't take any chance that the government would find out and be waiting for us at the airport and not allow us to leave."
▲▲▲▲▲▲

to Miami [Florida], and getting used to living in the United States was a culture shock like you wouldn't believe." Cristina attended Assumption Academy in Miami. It was another Catholic school, but it was not nearly as strict as *Esclavas del Corazón Sagrado*. With blond hair and green eyes, Cristina looked like a typical American girl. But even small differences didn't escape the notice of her new classmates, and at the time, one of Cristina's differences was her pierced ears. "They treated us like we were savages," she remembers. "The American kids would come up to me and say, 'Man, your ears are pierced. Do you people pierce your noses too?'" The kids also asked me questions like, "Do you have air conditioning or refrigerators in Cuba?" To this Cristina thought, "Don't they have school in the United States? Didn't these kids learn about other countries besides their own?"

Cristina at 14 years old, taken in Miami, Florida

Her favorite subjects in school included English and creative writing, which seems natural since her parents and grandparents were publishers. But it was during these first years that she also began to keep a journal, where she would write about her feelings and the things she couldn't talk about. "My family had just arrived [in the U.S.]. They had a lot of different jobs and a lot of stress," she explains. "When you leave your country under those circumstances, the kids [wonder], 'Who can I talk to?' I didn't have a counselor, I didn't have Mrs. Rogers. [The journal] was all I could trust. I started my journal when I was twelve and it saved my life."

There were other painful culture clashes that Cristina remembers. Young Latinas are raised to give a kiss on each cheek when greeting people as a sign of affection and, with adults, as a sign of respect. At age twelve, Cristina attended a birthday party for one of her school friends. It was her first party in the U.S. She ran and embraced her friend, giving her a kiss on each cheek. The parents all looked at her as if she'd suddenly grown another head.

Getting older didn't seem to help matters, either. As a teenager, she remembers standing in a corner with her cousins, too frightened to move when they realized that they were at a party with boys and the parents were gone. "Their parents would drop them off and the kids would dance cheek to cheek and start necking. We were terrified. We didn't have that. In Cuba, we had a system called chaperones. When you date, you take a brother or a sister or a parent with you. You would sit with your boyfriend in the movies and they [the chaperones] would sit behind you."

▼▼▼▼▼

"My new classmates treated us like we were savages. The American kids would come up to me and say, 'Man, your ears are pierced. Do you people pierce your noses, too?'"

▲▲▲▲▲

▼▼▼▼▼▼

Her dream
was to
become a
bilingual
journalist.

▲▲▲▲▲▲

Cristina's parents were not about to let that tradition go. The Saralegui family luckily had Aunt Tita, who followed Cristina on dates until she was twenty. "My boyfriend would pick me up and it would be us, another couple, and my aunt. At the dance she would not sit at the table. She would follow me to the dance floor and stand at the edge to make sure that the boy did not do anything improper." Aunt Tita, who never married, was in her sixties at the time.

Following in the family business, Cristina pursued a journalism degree at the University of Miami. Though she was taking classes for print journalism, her dream was to become a bilingual journalist, and in order to do this she had to learn to write in Spanish. In her last year in college she was required to take an internship. She applied for and won an internship at *Vanidades* magazine. By this time, her family had sold the magazine, so she had had to talk to the editor, a Colombian lady, Elvira Mendoza, to ask for the job. She was offered a position in the photo morgue (where publications keep photos filed), but the test to get the job required her to identify a certain picture. "Who is this?" Mendoza asked her. "Senator Teddy Kennedy," Cristina replied. She got the job.

Eventually Cristina began writing articles for the magazine. She wrote the first two in English, which then had to be translated into Spanish. After that, Mendoza advised her, "Either learn how to write in Spanish or I'm going to have to

CRISTINA SARALEGUI

CRISTINA SARALEGUI

Cristina was hired as a writer for *Cosmopolitan en Español*. Six years later, she became the editor in chief.

replace you because I can't afford to pay you and a translator." She did learn, but she had to teach herself. She bought a book of Spanish synonyms and a Spanish-English dictionary. "I started writing in Spanish and that is why I have the career I have today." She stayed in print journalism for twenty-five years. She never earned her degree, however, though she was only nine credits short. Her parents were having financial problems at the time, and they were trying to keep her brother at a private military school while sending Cristina to the university. In the end, her father opted to take Cristina out of college rather than take her brother out of military school. "My father told me, 'Your brother will have to support a wife someday, but you, you are not my responsibility. You're your husband's.' So, because my father was such a *machista*, I didn't finish my college degree." But, she adds, "I have since forgiven him."

Her journalism career took root at *Vanidades*. Year after year she received more authority, becoming a writer and eventually an editor. *Vanidades* was owned by Editorial America, which publishes several magazines. In 1973, the company launched *Cosmopolitan en Español*, a Spanish-language beauty magazine that targeted Latinas, and Cristina was hired as a writer. It was the Spanish version of the American magazine *Cosmopolitan*. Six years later, she became the magazine's editor in chief.

CRISTINA SARALEGUI

While working for *Cosmopolitan en Español*, Cristina met the editor of *Cosmopolitan*, Helen Gurley Brown, a woman who became Cristina's professional mentor. "She [Gurley Brown] taught me a lot about being a working woman," asserts Cristina. "She shaped my life as a professional woman."

As a feminist, Gurley Brown believes that women should be treated as equals to men, but in order for that to happen, she doesn't suggest that women become men. In the pages of *Cosmopolitan*, she stressed that women should be accepted as equals to men, on their own terms. At the time that Cristina was working for the magazine, *Cosmopolitan* had been around for over 100 years, but it had become stale and didn't reflect the changing attitudes of women in the 1970s. Cristina, meanwhile, had been raised to believe that women should be seen and not heard. They should be ladylike, beautiful, and traditional. She still admires Gurley Brown because, she says, "What she established [at *Cosmopolitan*] was part of the sexual revolution—that women had a right to their sexuality. Coming from Cuba, it blew my mind that somebody like Helen would actually go public and fight for that."

As Cristina progressed in her job at *Cosmopolitan en Español*, she also accepted freelance work outside the magazine. She eventually found freelance work with Univision. In 1989, the president of the company, Joaquín

▼▼▼▼▼▼
In 1989, Cristina was offered a new job. It was on television, working for the Univision network.
▲▲▲▲▲▲

CRISTINA SARALEGUI

Television sign language took some getting used to.

Blaya, offered her a new job. He told her, "I can double your salary with this one job and you can let go of the other six." Her simple response was, "I'm coming." At that moment, the girl who was raised to be a print journalist made the leap into television. She became the host of her own program, *El Show de Cristina*.

Being in front of a camera was not the hard part, she says. She had been on television before. As the editor of an international women's magazine, she was asked fairly often to go on TV and talk about women's issues. It was television sign language that took getting used to. Because the cameras are on and the show is taping, cameramen signal a television personality in order to communicate. They tell the personality when it's time to go to a commercial, when to speed up and get to the end of an interview, or when time is up and the interview has to end. About taping the first show of *El Show de Cristina*, she says, "I was so nervous. I didn't know how to read hand signals and television is all hand signals—it's like a football game. I had never read a TelePrompTer. So the first day, I had five cameras on me and a microphone in my hand and I was sweating so badly I thought, 'My God, can this thing electrocute me?'" She survived, and within six months *El Show de Cristina* was rated number one in its time slot. It has stayed there ever since.

The popularity of television talk shows exploded in the early 1990s. So many new talk shows were introduced that competition for ratings encouraged each show to be more outrageous than the next. Televised on Univision and in Spanish, *El Show de Cristina* is spared the head-to-head competition with the other shows, which allows it to be different. Cristina's show tends to take a more respectful tone toward its guests and its audience, and today, as the show's producer as well as its host, Cristina says she does this deliberately. She believes that the success of her show is due to her objective that the show educate as well as entertain. "If you promote people screaming at each other, like some of the newer talk shows, what you get is a henhouse. You don't get anything across.

Cristina wants her show to be educational as well as entertaining.

CRISTINA SARALEGUI

Whenever things get out of control, I stop the taping and wait until the animals quiet down, and then we start again. If people can't hear, they can't learn. Nobody would ever throw a chair on my show; it would never air."

Because there are few Latino television personalities to look up to, Cristina is very aware of her responsibility as a celebrity. She says that she chooses topics that "promote things that are going to help Latinos as a whole." When the state of California passed Proposition 187, which denies many social services, including an education, to the children of illegal immigrants, Cristina decided to discuss it on her show. Taped in Miami, *Cristina* (as the show is called today) has a mostly Cuban-American studio audience, who, when asked about Proposition 187, said, "That's a Mexican problem." On the show, Cristina responded, "This is not a Mexican problem. This is a problem we're all going to have to face." Eventually, several states, including Florida, and then Congress began to introduce legislation similar to Proposition 187, targeting illegal Latino immigrants. In order for Latinos to fight attacks like these and progress as a community, Cristina says, "We have to identify what it is to be Hispanic or Latino here [in the U.S.], and we have to stop fighting about semantics. I have actually been present in places where people go at each other's throats because of [the question] 'Are we Latinos or are we Hispanics?' So here are these people debating all

▼▼▼▼▼▼

Cristina likes to choose show topics that "promote things that are going to help Latinos as a whole."

▲▲▲▲▲▲

this baloney when what they have to be is *apoyando* (supporting each other)."

Besides discussing important social issues on her show, Cristina has taken on a personal cause: educating Latinos about AIDS. She chose this cause for several reasons. When the show first began, Cristina says she became more aware of all the trouble in the world, and it affected her deeply. She became so concerned that she says she saw a psychologist to help her learn to separate herself from her show. But when a close friend of hers, who had been married for several years, contracted HIV, the virus that causes AIDS, Cristina invited her to be on the show. She asked her how a heterosexual woman could contract AIDS, and her friend told her that her husband

Cristina does not allow a lot of yelling and screaming on her show, because she feels she doesn't get anything accomplished that way.

had contracted the disease from another woman and had never told her. It was only after he died that his family told her about his affair. Cristina's friend and her friend's daughter were then tested, and both were positive for HIV.

"I started studying AIDS among Hispanics," Cristina says. "I realized that we, especially

Cristina prefers to do shows that make her laugh instead of ones that make her cry. However, she's most proud of the shows that deal with serious issues.

women, were the highest statistic and that there's a lot of urban Hispanic men who are bisexual and do not use protection [a condom]." The mother of three, with two of them teenagers (Cristina Amalia, 19; Stephanie, 15; and Jon, 11), Cristina was also concerned about informing younger Latinos about the danger of AIDS. "I realized that the only weapon you can give kids is information. You can give them a condom, but if you don't tell them why, they won't use it. Teenagers feel invincible. I started teaching my own kids, and then I started a whole series of shows that was called Up With Life."

Culturally, Latinos are uncomfortable discussing certain topics, and at the top of the list are sickness and sex. As part of her campaign, Cristina pairs a teenager who is HIV positive with someone the same age who is not. The two discuss the disease, sex, and the importance of using protection. On one show, she invited two boys, one fifteen and the other sixteen, who had been sexually active since the age of thirteen and who believed that because the girls with whom they had had unprotected sex were so young, they could not possibly have AIDS. She then paired one of the boys with a boy who was sixteen but who had learned he was HIV positive when he turned fourteen. He told the boy how, like him, he believed that because he and his partners were young he could not get AIDS, and how he regrets that he didn't protect himself.

CRISTINA SARALEGUI

Cristina admits that she prefers to do shows that make her laugh instead of ones that make her cry, but she's most proud of the shows that deal with serious issues like AIDS. On her most compelling show, Cristina invited the father of Pedro Zamora, one of the first Latinos to star on the MTV program *The Real World*, to come on her show. Pedro, who had contracted AIDS and who eventually died from the disease, had been a guest on *Cristina* several times. "When we met Pedro Zamora, he represented the young man that all Hispanic mothers and fathers want to have," remembers Cristina. "He was beautiful, strong, respectful, a good student, and a good role model." In order to show how important it is to communicate with kids, Pedro's father admitted that he had made a mistake with his children. "I took care of my girls," he said. "I told everybody, 'The girls stay in the house, the boys will learn in the streets.' I did not discuss with him about safe sex. I did not feel comfortable discussing his [Pedro's] homosexuality. I was just a Hispanic father, I was rigid, and that cost me my son's life."

Cristina plans to take her Up With Life campaign on a nationwide tour to help encourage discussion of this disease in Latino communities. "I'm also working on a project to raise funds to help those in the Hispanic population that don't have the money to afford the new drugs for AIDS," she says.

As a Latina, Cristina believes it's important to pass her heritage on to her children.

Cristina has no plans to go back to Cuba. She has no family left there, and she does not want to support Castro in any shape or form.

CRISTINA SARALEGUI

Full of plans for the future, Cristina doesn't spend much time looking back, although that frightened little Mati is still with her. As a Latina, she believes it's very important to pass on her Hispanic heritage to her children. She's told them a lot about Cuba, what her life there was like, and how life has changed so drastically for the Cubans who stayed. "I think every single Cuban-American kid that grows up in the United States has [Cuba] imbedded in his mind. As parents, we cannot let that die," Cristina insists. "We have to explain to them where they came from, and even though they're not going back—most of them— you have to always keep your country in your mind." She, however, has no plans to go back, not even to visit. No Saralegui family member remains there, and her feelings toward the country's dictator, Castro, won't allow her to consider it. "I don't want to go back. I do not want to give American dollars to Castro," she emphasizes. "I don't want to support his regime in any shape or form. I don't want to go there until Castro leaves . . . or dies."

For now she's happy in her career and with her family, although she admits, "The least enjoyable aspect of my career is the lack of privacy and time. It seems like I'm always in a hurry." Cristina's daughter Cristina Amalia is from her first marriage. Stephanie is her stepdaughter, the daughter of her second husband, Marcos Avila, and his first wife. Jon is the son of Cristina and Avila. Her husband was a founding member of Miami Sound Machine, Gloria and Emilio Estefan's band. She met Avila while visiting the Estefans in Peru. They were married on June 9, 1984. According to Cristina, "I met Marcos, and our lives changed forever. Further down the road, when I started my television show, Marcos became my manager, and he handles all the business for our company."

Her future plans include finding more time to write. Cristina has never completely left her first love, print journalism. She co-publishes *Cristina La Revista,* a monthly magazine printed in Spanish. Her autobiography, *My Life as a Blonde,* will be published in March 1998 (Warner Books). "My magazine gives me an opportunity to explore in depth many subjects I can only touch on in television and radio. I want to try to improve the lives of Hispanic Americans to help them become more productive members of their communities." True to her word, Cristina takes every opportunity to do just that. Whether it's on her show, in her magazine, or on speaking tours, Cristina Saralegui provides her audience, family, and friends with something about which to think and of which to be proud.

Cristina likes to explore many subjects relevant to Latinos on her show and in her magazine.

TRENT DIMAS

Olympic Gymnast, Public Speaker
1970–

"**P**erseverance takes one beyond a simple goal. It will take you, as it does me, to places [you think are] only in dreams. "

Trent Dimas, as told to Valerie Menard, October 1996

BIO HIGHLIGHTS

- Born November 10, 1970, in Albuquerque, New Mexico; mother: Bonnie Rivera; father: Ted Dimas Sr.
- Traveled across the country with parents, evangelizing
- 1975, took first community center gymnastics class
- Educated by his parents at home until seventh grade
- Attended Eisenhower Middle School in Albuquerque
- 1989, graduated from El Dorado High School
- Received full scholarship to the University of Nebraska
- 1990, member of the NCAA National Championship gymnastics team; three-time All-American
- 1992, became a member of the U.S. Gymnastics Team at the Barcelona Olympics and won a gold medal on the high bar in the event finals
- Retired from gymnastics and became a public speaker and role model for young people
- December 29, 1996, married Lisa Harris
- Currently, attending the University of Denver

TRENT DIMAS

When Trent Dimas stepped up to compete on the high bar in the event finals of the 1992 Olympics in Barcelona, Spain, he had already set a precedent. Watching this young, handsome Latino from Albuquerque, New Mexico, provided the first time in Olympic history that one could see a Latino gymnast compete as a member of an American team. What he proceeded to do on the high bar would also make history.

Trent Dimas is the first Latino gymnast to win an Olympic gold medal on an American team.

The high bar (or horizontal bar), which stands nine feet from the ground, is considered the most dangerous event in men's gymnastics. A gymnast is continually moving and swinging and performs not only balance moves such as handstands but also release moves, where he actually lets go of the bar, hurls himself above it, and then catches it as he descends. In competition, the more release moves a gymnast successfully performs adds to his score. Trent Dimas perfectly performed three of these, including a

Kovacs (two somersaults above the bar) and a Tkatchev Gienger (a somersault with one half twist re-grasp). His final move, the dismount, was a triple somersault. The only element left to complete for a good score was his landing, and in the Olympics, you must land without taking a step. Dimas stuck the landing.

As he raised his hand to signal the end of his routine, his face broke into a huge smile. He knew it was the best routine he'd ever performed. "After I stuck the dismount, I didn't want to move," he said. "I wanted to make sure the judges saw that I had stuck my routine." They did and rewarded Dimas with a score of 9.875 (a score of 10 is considered perfect) and an Olympic gold medal. At that moment, Trent Dimas became the first U.S. gymnast, male or female, to win a gold medal in a non-boycotted (every country competed) Olympics in 60 years. As of 1996, he has been the only Latino to achieve this.

Trent Dimas was born in Albuquerque, New Mexico, on November 10, 1970, to Ted Sr., a masonry contractor and former flyweight Golden Gloves boxing champion, and Bonnie Rivera Dimas. Trent is of Spanish, French, and Greek ethnicity, and although he doesn't speak Spanish, both his parents do. He has a brother, Ted Jr., who is two

Trent at three years old

years older than he. Trent says his mother stayed home and took care of the family when he was a boy. She later managed a hotel. Both parents are devout Christians and traveled across the country with the boys as evangelists. His parents met as youngsters; the Rivera and Dimas families lived next door to each other. Both families were

so close that not only did Ted and Bonnie marry, but Ted's brother and Bonnie's sister also eventually married. Ted and Bonnie became ministers of the Christian faith. Trent remembers that though they traveled a lot, the immediate family unit of four remained very close. "My parents have always looked after us very well; they never let us out of their sight. They put their arms around us and never let anything of the outside world into our close-knit family," he says. Trent is also impressed with the interest his parents took in him and his brother and the time that they devoted to them. "They took time out of every day to explain and experience the world around us, which taught us that we were special, important kids. My dad took us to job sites and showed us how he made money. Ted Jr. and I were very young when we learned the meaning of *making a living.*"

Ted (left) and Trent (right) have always been close friends.

For religious reasons and to maintain control over their education, Bonnie and Ted decided to educate Ted Jr. and Trent at home. Now more popular and widely accepted, home schooling in the 1970s and 1980s when Ted and Trent were taught was an innovative concept. It worked well for several reasons. The boys spent a great deal of time at home, they were able to travel together, and then, later, they were able to schedule their gymnastics training around their home lessons. Trent's father taught them math and science, while his mother taught them English and social studies; they continued to do so until his brother entered high school and Trent entered seventh grade. While they were being educated at home, his parents enrolled them in community sports programs so that the boys could meet and play with other children their age. Says Trent, "Our parents knew the importance of making friends and socializing with kids our own age. They made sure we did constructive activities while we played." He attended Eisenhower Middle School and El Dorado High School, both in Albuquerque.

Ted (front left) with Trent (behind) and their mother and father, taken in 1981

Along with memories of traveling with his parents, Trent's early memories are connected to gymnastics. He began his gymnastics career at the young age of five, along with his brother. The boys also played soccer together, coached

TRENT DIMAS

by their parents. When he considers how he chose to pursue gymnastics, he says, "It just fell into my lap." One year the state soccer championships and the state gymnastics meet were scheduled on the same weekend. "Our parents let us make the decision," he says. "We picked gymnastics." Thinking further about the choice, Trent admits that there might have been a bit more to it. He was naturally attracted to gymnastics because it's considered an individual sport, which makes the athlete more responsible for his or her success. "I love competing," he says. "Gymnastics encourages discipline. It encourages you to set goals and to learn to confront adversity, whether it's physical pain or mental weakness."

Because both boys competed in the same sports, Trent claims it worked to his advantage.

Trent could perform for the camera, too.

Rather than holding Ted Jr. back so that Trent could catch up, their father pushed Trent to be as good as his brother. "My parents never liked to split us up. They pushed me to be as strong and as skilled as Ted, and that helped me out quite a bit," he says. In high school, although his main focus was still gymnastics and it was through gymnastics that he was able to travel all over the world, Trent remembers having the typical worries of most high school kids. He worried about missing football games, not playing football, and not participating in the usual activities associated with high school. "But by the time I got a little older, I realized that competing for the United States as a top athlete was an incredible honor."

Constantly supported and encouraged by his parents, Trent appreciates the sacrifices they made to make sure the boys could compete in gymnastics. There was not much money, but there was also little time for the boys' attention to wander or for them to develop bad habits. "My parents were always with us, at competitions, at school, everywhere. They also made it clear that they would support whatever we wanted to pursue, but that we couldn't quit once we started. Finishing was important."

The brothers continued to compete together, and when it came time to choose a college, Trent chose the University of Nebraska, the same university his brother was already attending. "In 1989, I was a blue chip recruit and

▼▼▼▼▼

"My parents pushed me to be as strong and as skilled as Ted, and that helped me out quite a bit."

▲▲▲▲▲▲

TRENT DIMAS

had been offered a full scholarship to any college in the United States that had a gymnastics program," he explains. "Though all of them had much to offer, nobody could offer what the University of Nebraska could—my brother." Ted was attending on a full athletic scholarship. He had already completed two years. "This was the reason I finally chose Nebraska."

Trent was already competing for the United States Senior National Team. He joined Ted on the NCAA level for the Nebraska Cornhuskers. He enrolled at the university and planned to earn a marketing degree. That year, the Cornhuskers became number one in gymnastics and won the 1990 National Team

Trent joined Ted at the University of Nebraska, and the two brothers competed on the NCAA level for the Nebraska Cornhuskers.

Championships. But after only one year, Trent surprised everyone and left.

"Even though I was only at the University of Nebraska for one year, my memories of college are incredible," he says. "My education was very important to me, and it was a lot different from high school. People were there to learn because they chose to, and you took classes that you wanted to take instead of classes that you had to take."

Gymnastics is a very demanding sport. To be competitive, an athlete must train every day and, at the same time, avoid injury. The intense pressure of competition also takes a daily toll on self-confidence. Gymnasts compete in at least two national and five international tournaments annually. Each time they watch others perform, they notice new techniques and skills that will take the competition to a higher, more difficult level. Trent saw his dream of being an Olympic athlete getting closer and closer, and he knew he had to make the right choice to make it happen. After one year at the University of Nebraska, he opted to return to his hometown gym, Gold Cup Gymnastics in Albuquerque, and train with his lifelong coach, Ed Burch. According to Trent, he had reached a fork in the road of his career, and he had to choose the right path. As he puts it, "I remember watching Lance Ringaid in the American Cup in 1990, and I thought, 'Wow, this is the guy who I trained with for so many years, and he's really surpassing me

Trent saw his dream of being an Olympic athlete getting closer and closer, and he knew he had to make the right choice to make it happen.

in skill.' I started to think about where my gymnastics career was going. I needed the most effective training to prepare for the Olympic team. With only two years to go, I needed to train full time, be around more great athletes, and get more one-on-one coaching."

An athlete competes against more than just other athletes. Trent was successful in his early gymnastics career, and he struggled to maintain top form. He was too tall (he is 5'10", when the average height for male gymnasts was 5'5"), he had unusually long arms, and he had to do extra strength exercises to gain needed muscles. As he got older, his body was not an advantage. In an interview with the *Davis County [State] Clipper*, he said, "Before I was a senior in high school, I had been to half the countries in the world. I never was the number-one guy on the team. I was always just hanging in there at fifth or sixth. I was a gymnast of national merit, but not the best all-arounder. It all came out in Barcelona."

The road to Barcelona and the 1992 Olympics was not easy. Because he had left the gymnastics program at the University of Nebraska, which was run by the U.S. Gymnastics Team coach, Trent was considered a dark horse when he entered the U.S. Olympic trials. When he left his scholarship to train full time, he also suffered a loss of financial support. At the age of 20, Trent was paying his own way. A gymnastics fan who had seen Trent on television vying for a spot on the national team was

The road to Barcelona was not easy. Trent was considered a dark horse when he entered the U.S. Olympic trials.

inspired by his dedication. He sent him a check to help with living expenses. This person was George Steinbrenner, owner of the New York Yankees. Trent was able to continue training.

Even though he was bothered by an injury at the time of the trials, Trent unexpectedly qualified. He still wasn't considered a medal hopeful. In Barcelona, he was the first American to compete in almost every event, sent out to provide the base score for everyone else to top. "I was very upset when I saw the lineup," says Burch. "The only problem I had [was that] he got up in the first rotation. He had the best compulsory meet of his life."

During his stay in Barcelona, Trent says he was determined to experience everything about the Olympics. Just being an Olympian had satisfied his ultimate goal; everything else that he achieved would just be extra. He toured the city, interacting with other athletes and the people of Barcelona. "Many on the men's gymnastics team stayed in their rooms and passed the time playing cards. I figured that I would never be on another Olympic team, so I told myself that while I was in Barcelona, I was going to have some fun. I spent my free time with athletes from other countries, touring, shopping, and generally being in awe of being a part of the American team. There was a true Olympic spirit throughout that city." Even today, Trent says that Barcelona is one of his favorite cities in the world.

During his stay in Barcelona, Trent says he was determined to experience everything about the Olympics.

TRENT DIMAS

Trent was one of the eight best high bar gymnasts competing in the Olympic Games.

Nineteen ninety-two was not a good year for the men's U.S. Gymnastics Team. Although favored to possibly win a medal, it finished fifth in the team competition. The second round of competition determines the best all-around individual, the single male gymnast with the top score after competing in all six events: the parallel bars, the floor exercise, the rings, the pommel horse, the vault, and the high bar. After three days of gymnastics, the third and final round of competition, the event finals, awards the individual gymnast who performs best on each apparatus. Trent Dimas found himself in the event finals competing on the high bar.

Trent was preparing to perform in the most important competition the sport of gymnastics had to offer. He was one of the eight best high bar gymnasts competing in the Olympic Games. Every country was represented in this Olympics, including the ever-powerful Unified Team, which had always dominated internationally. Trent was now competing for a medal.

On the first night, he thought, "I can win the gold medal." But that thought was soon replaced by, "Maybe I could win a silver," and then, "Maybe I could win a bronze," and finally, "I made the top eight and that's good enough." So before the final competition began, he had settled on just being satisfied with having made the event finals at all. But his coach, Ed Burch, had other plans. "We worked to peak (make him be in the best shape possible) Trent in Barcelona," he explains. Though Dimas's position as the first in every rotation didn't help that plan, Burch said, referring to when he heard that Dimas had made the event finals, "I was pretty confident in Trent that he would win a medal."

Up on the bar, Trent showed poise as well as ability. His body, he says, seemed to go into automatic as he successfully performed each move. "My body was doing the work," he

Trent performed a near-perfect routine on the high bar in Barcelona.

TRENT DIMAS

remembers, "and my mind was off in another world, saying, 'I can't believe this is happening.'" He was once called a dark horse, but Trent performed the best routine of his life when he needed to. On this day in 1992 in Barcelona, Trent Dimas was definitely on.

It was, nevertheless, a new experience for him. Even on his way to the platform to have the medal put around his neck, Trent walked past the spot where the gold medalist stands. Silver medalist Grigory Misiutin of the Unified Team (Russia) nudged Trent into the gold-medal position.

When all the scores were posted, Trent and his coach, Ed Burch (left) could hardly believe he'd won a gold medal.

TRENT DIMAS

TRENT DIMAS

"The men's [gymnastics] program needed a hero," says Burch of Trent's victory. "We've been put down a lot. We needed a hero like Trent."

After receiving the gold medal, Trent says one of his fondest memories of the experience happened that night. After the entire British team took him out to celebrate, he spent some time alone, walking on the beach and just thinking about what being an Olympian meant. "I was going over the fact that I had surpassed my goal of being an Olympic team member by actually earning a medal, a gold medal," he says. "I was overwhelmed with USA pride."

Trent stopped training after Barcelona. He was successful in gaining contracts with ten corporations, including Kodak, McDonald's, IBM, Xerox, AT&T, and Visa. Promotions, public speaking, and appearances filled up much of his time. But as the 1996 Olympic Games in Atlanta drew near, he felt the call to compete one last time. This road to the Olympics was even tougher than before. He began training in the spring of 1995, but his body would not cooperate. Four months before the 1996 trials, during a daily training session, the grip on his right hand caught as he tried to release from the rings. Dangling by one arm from the apparatus, and with a sharp pain and burning sensation through his wrist, he had to pull himself up to detach himself. That injury never completely healed, and before the 1996 Olympic trials, he

After Trent won the gold medal, the entire British team took him out to celebrate.

also suffered a back injury. In a February 4, 1996, interview with *The Denver Post*, he says, "It's always been a tough road for me. Sometime I'd like to be in top condition to see what I can do,

Trent received contracts with several corporations, such as Kodak, to endorse their products.

" LAUGH AT GRAVITY. REMEMBER YOUR TRAINING. MAKE ADJUSTMENTS. TAKE A CHANCE. USE GREAT FILM. EMBRACE DESTINY. "

© Eastman Kodak Company, 1996

WHAT FILM IS IN YOUR CAMERA?

CHRIS COLE ON PHOTOGRAPHING TRENT DIMAS, '92 OLYMPICS —

Kodak

TRENT DIMAS

where I stand." He's never had another opportunity.

Making the 1996 Olympic team may not have been his destiny, but Trent has other plans to keep him busy. On December 29, 1996, he married Lisa Harris, his girlfriend of many years. Fatefully, he first met Lisa in seventh grade, the first year he attended public school. They dated during their high school and college years before deciding to marry. During that time, Lisa completed a bachelor's degree in health education. "My relationship with Lisa has been truly wonderful," he says. "She has been supportive of me following my dreams despite

Lisa and Trent at their wedding reception with Lisa's father all the complications. She always makes me laugh, even when the situation seems hopeless. [She's] someone I've always been able to talk to. Every day is a new adventure, and I love having her as my friend and wife." He and Lisa also share a love of outdoor sports such as skiing and mountain biking. Trent also loves watching movies and boasts that he's the world's best movie critic. "We just plain have a lot of fun together."

His professional goals may keep him tied to gymnastics, but Trent has personal, spiritual goals he pursues with the same enthusiasm, such as being a role model to young people. Unlike many professional athletes who reject the title "role model," Dimas embraces it. "I like being a role model because I feel people who are constantly faced with decisions, always getting up when they fall, and those who are trying to improve are the best role models. I always wonder why some athletes complain about kids who want an autograph, for example. You fight all your life for somebody to even want your autograph, and when you get there, [some athletes think] it's too much of a hassle. I've always tried to get away from being your stereotypical athlete."

Trent has adopted many causes, but the one closest to his heart is Children's Hospice International, an organization that works with terminally ill children. "Working with ill children and seeing how their lives are—it can really

▼▼▼▼▼

"I like being a role model because I feel people who are constantly faced with decisions, always getting up when they fall, and those who are trying to improve are the best role models."

Trent Dimas

bring you back to Earth," he explains. "These kids don't ask for anything special . . . these kids are just looking forward to having a completely normal day. CHI is probably the organization that has made me appreciate what athletics has done in my life. Plus, I get to share the prestige of winning the medal with others."

But Trent doesn't stop there. He also shares the prestige of the medal with children all over the country, from those who attend private schools to those who are at risk of dropping out of school. He carries his gold medal with him to inspire children to believe in their dreams and know that they can come true. "I want these kids to be able to touch it and to see that it is a reality. If they work hard and have goals and have dedication, it can happen for them," he says. On his speaking tours, Trent says he finds that many children are surprised to learn that there actually is a process for being successful. His job, he says, is to encourage their goals, but he likes to add a little realistic advice as well. "I try to tell [the kids] that there's no easy way. They ask me how much money I make, and I tell them, 'You can't have ulterior motives like that. You've got to be able to put in the hours and take baby steps to get to your ultimate goal.' I love watching a kid's face, who more than likely believes that all I had to do was go work out for a few months and hop on a plane to the Olympics to win. I explain how I trained for twenty years, attempting to qualify in

Trent has adopted many causes, but the one closest to his heart is Children's Hospice International.

three different Olympics. I only got one chance to prove myself. There is a lot of defeat involved with being successful. I understand that the Olympic champion title is easy for others to remember, but my entire career has been an experience."

The Dimas formula for success also includes accepting adversity and turning it into a challenge to be overcome. One of the key lessons he learned in his long gymnastics career, from the physical challenges of working through injuries and pain or the spiritual challenge of overcoming the disappointment of not performing well at a meet, has been dealing with adversity. He tells students, "There are going to be a lot of things in your way along the road. My mom used to always tell me that for every no there's a yes, and you have to keep knocking on the doors until you find where that yes is."

Trent is also a spokesman for the National Hispanic Scholarship Fund (NHSF), which in 1994 distributed $3 million in scholarships among 2,531 college-bound Hispanic students nationwide. "So many fundraisers just pay the people organizing the fund. Most of the money never reaches the people who need it," Trent says. "The NHSF turns around and gives ninety-five percent of the funds that they raise to the students who need it most." His support for the NHSF is so strong that he has arranged to send five students to college through scholarships in his name.

Trent is a spokesman for the National Hispanic Scholarship Fund.

TRENT DIMAS

Corporations, youth groups, and charities find a great spokesman and motivational speaker in Trent, who promotes fitness and good health. He's taken on a particular cause that speaks directly to teens: violence among young people. In a series of television public service announcements produced by the United States Olympic Committee (USOC), Trent discusses youth suicide. In the announcement, he encourages everyone to listen when a friend threatens suicide and to help them find help by calling a suicide prevention hotline. He also participates in the Champions in Life program, also sponsored by the USOC. Champions in Life sends Olympic athletes on tours to schools nationwide as role models for children, encouraging them to pursue becoming Olympians. Trent says that he sees few young Latinos competing in gymnastics junior programs. "Gymnastics is a progressive sport, and to be an elite gymnast, one has to begin training early in life. In order for more Hispanics to be in the Games, more must train hard as children with the focus of being in an Olympic Games as the primary goal."

Trent's future plans are pretty simple. He went back to school (this time at the University of Denver) to finish what he had begun. He will complete his degree and continue to prepare for

Trent met with President George Bush and the first lady.

a television career. Eventually, he and Lisa would like to start a family. At a very young age, Trent accomplished what many older male gymnasts still dream of achieving. As he continues to set personal goals, his future accomplishments will rise above his Olympic moment. Committed to sharing his achievements with others, he will touch the lives of many youngsters, and they will touch his gold medal. His message to them is this: "Perseverance takes one beyond a simple goal. It will take you, as it does me, to places [you think are] only in dreams."

Trent continues to set personal goals. His future accomplishments, he hopes, will rise above his Olympic moment.

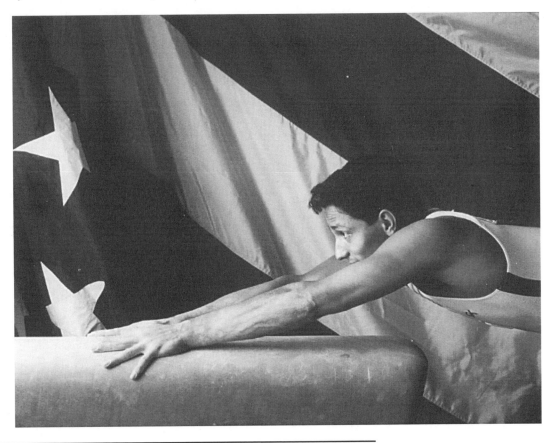

NYDIA VELÁZQUEZ

Congresswoman from New York's 12th District
1953–

"The most important thing for any human being is to have faith in himself or herself. If you don't have faith in yourself, you cannot expect other people to believe that you can do it. And also, be determined. Whenever you want to do something, just focus on that and go for it! Don't let others change your mind, saying, 'No, you can't do this.'

"Whatever you want to become in life—Yes, you can do it—what it takes is determination and faith in yourself. Focus on the things you want to accomplish. **"**

The Honorable Nydia M. Velázquez,
as told to Melanie Cole, November 20, 1996

BIO HIGHLIGHTS

- Born Nydia Margarita Velázquez March 28, 1953, in Yabucoa, Puerto Rico; mother: Carmen Luisa Serrano; father: Benito Velázquez
- Enrolled at age sixteen at the University of Puerto Rico in Rio Piedras, from which she graduated in 1974
- Earned master's degree in political science in 1976 from New York University and taught at Hunter College of the City University of New York
- 1984, first Latina appointed to serve on New York City Council
- 1986, appointed by the governor of Puerto Rico to serve as Secretary of the Department of Puerto Rican Community Affairs in the U.S.
- Elected as first Puerto Rican Congresswoman on November 5, 1992, representing New York's newly formed 12th District (Brooklyn, Manhattan, and Queens)
- Reelected to second term in 1994, and third term in 1996

Nydia Velázquez

Nydia was raised in a small wooden house in Puerto Rico, in the middle of sugarcane fields.

▲▲▲▲▲▲

Nydia Margarita Velázquez was born on March 28, 1953, to a working-class couple living on the outside edge of Yabucoa, Puerto Rico. Yabucoa is a small town on the Río Limones on the southeast corner of the island of Puerto Rico. What had brought the Velázquez family to this part of the island was its location as part of the sugarcane industry. In the first half of this century, Puerto Rico's economy was linked mainly to the agricultural crops of coffee, sugar, and tobacco.

The island of Puerto Rico is quite small, about the size of the state of Connecticut. It is a commonwealth of the United States, and its residents are U.S. citizens. In 1993 the people of Puerto Rico narrowly rejected a vote to become the fifty-first state. The government and the issues of the island, and of the Puerto Rican community that has settled on the mainland, have been important to Nydia Velázquez throughout her life.

Nydia and her twin sister, Magda, along with their seven other brothers and sisters, were raised in a small wooden house in the middle of the sugarcane fields. Nydia's brothers and other sisters are Juan, Roberto, Rafael, Carmen, Luz, Luis, and Maria.

Nydia's father, Benito Velázquez, was born on the island in 1913 and, when his children were small, earned his living principally as a sugarcane cutter. Benito, who had a third-grade education, later became a butcher and the owner of a legal cock-fighting business. Throughout his life, two things were constant: his love for his family and his ability as a political organizer. He was an extremely powerful speaker who could rally his fellow workers to fight for their rights as hired employees of large sugar corporations based in Puerto Rico.

Nydia remembers that when her father would come back from work or his meetings, and in the morning before the children went off to school, he would say the same thing. "He was—every day—lecturing us: 'Remember this. I am a poor person, and I cannot leave you with any money. The only thing, the only legacy that I can leave you, is to get your education.' He was saying this every single day," says Nydia. "He instilled in us the value of education, to everyone in my family. He showed us that education was the key." As a result of this preaching, all of the Velázquez children were motivated and most attended college. The older brothers became entrepreneurs, one sister is an anesthesiologist, and another is a cosmetologist.

One of Benito's favorite activities was local politics. He was a champion of the working men and women of Puerto Rico and even founded a political party in Yabucoa. His strong social activism filtered down to his children, especially to Nydia, who remembers that dinner conversations were often about the rights of workers and other political issues. Nydia told a reporter for *The New York Times*, "I always

One of Benito's favorite activities was local politics. He was a champion of the working men and women of Puerto Rico.

▼▼▼▼▼▼

"I always wanted to be like my father," says Nydia.

▲▲▲▲▲▲

wanted to be like my father," and as a U.S. Congresswoman, she has stood up for the social issues championed by her father: better jobs, increased opportunities, and civil rights. Nydia is the only one of her family to devote her entire life to politics—first as a student and teacher of politics and later as an appointed and elected official, doing the "real work" of politics by representing her people.

Nydia's mother, Carmen Luisa (Serrano) Velázquez, born in 1922, supplemented the family income by selling a traditional Puerto Rican food, pasteles (pastries made of mashed root vegetables stuffed with meat and wrapped in plantain leaves), to the sugarcane cutters who worked in the nearby fields. Nydia remembers that it was her father, more than her mother, who challenged the children to make something of themselves beyond their small village, beyond the fields of sugarcane. She remembers that her mother had a different kind of strength. She kept everything going. "My mother was so involved in raising us—nine children! It was a lot of work!" Nydia says. "And she worked also on the farm, so she was too much involved doing the day-to-day work to get involved in intellectual discussions." She was the pragmatic one, while Nydia's father was the idealistic one, constantly instructing, "Things can be better. You can make them better."

Nydia remembers how hard it was growing up in the little house. One of her most vivid memories is of the entire family having to leave the house when the Río Limones flooded. Although Puerto Rico is normally warm and sunny year-round, during the torrential rainy seasons, families often have to flee the vicinity. "We had more than just the nine children and our parents living in the house," recalls Nydia. "There was a large extended family—of aunts and cousins—all living under the same roof. There were fourteen people sharing a three-bedroom house! What was really bad was we were at the mercy of the river. The Río Limones would flood. Whenever it flooded, we'd have to leave the house—all of us—and walk somewhere to a safe place. This would sometimes be in the middle of the night, two o'clock in the morning. We would get up and walk forty-five minutes to a relative's home."

Nydia's natural leadership abilities were clear even at a young age. She remembers that among family or in groups of friends, she always had a take-charge attitude. "When I was growing up in the family, I was the one organizing the games, making the decisions about what we would play that day and where to do it," Nydia says.

As the child of a poor cane-cutter, Nydia's life might have become one of manual labor and childbearing. Most of the children in the area toiled in the fields alongside their parents. If a family had more hands, it meant they could earn more at harvest time. But Nydia had other ideas.

▼▼▼▼▼▼
Nydia's natural leadership abilities were clear even at a young age. She had a take-charge attitude.
▲▲▲▲▲▲

NYDIA VELÁZQUEZ

Memories of her father's political involvement have propelled her throughout her life.

She was an extremely bright girl, and by the age of five, she begged her parents to let her go to school. So she was enrolled in Yabucoa's elementary school, *Secunda Unidad de Limones*.

She enjoyed school so much that she learned very quickly. She loved history classes, particularly those in which the students were encouraged to discuss issues and events. She learned how exciting it felt to get people to stand up for their beliefs. "When I was in the eighth grade," Nydia remembers, "in history class, sometimes I would say things that I really didn't believe, just to encourage other people to debate, to argue."

In encouraging this kind of debate, Nydia was practicing a skill that she had observed in her father's political meetings and that she would one day use as a college professor and on the floor of the U.S. House of Representatives. Indeed, memories of her father's political involvement have propelled her throughout her life. "My father used to have these big, huge meetings using flatbed trucks. In the family's patio—the backyard—300 people or 400 people would be gathering. And I saw politicians coming in, giving their speeches. I also observed my father speaking to the crowd, and even though he just went to school until . . . I think it was the third grade, he was very eloquent. He was a good, good speaker. So I was really very small, but I was paying a lot of attention to that. I remember telling myself, 'One day, I want to be like him.'"

Nydia Velázquez

Nydia was able to graduate from high school three years early, at the age of 15. This happened because she was enrolled in a gifted, self-paced program. Explains Nydia: "From eighth grade I was transferred to high school. But what I did once I got in high school was instead of four years, I finished it in two years, and this is how I started my first year in college when I was 16."

She was the first person in her immediate family to receive a college degree. While she had a boyfriend in high school, her parents did not encourage dating and, according to Nydia, dating and marriage were "not my interest" at that time. By the age of 16, she was already enrolled at the University of Puerto Rico in Rio Piedras.

In college, Nydia majored in political science. She chose this field because of her fascination with politics. She continued to excel academically, graduating magna cum laude (with very high honors) in 1974. That same year, she won a scholarship to continue her education in the United States. This caused a bit of worry in her family, particularly with her father. Nydia had always been close to her father, and he was reluctant to have her study so far away. But two of her professors talked him into accepting Nydia's decision, since it seemed her career had nowhere to go but up. So, with her family's reluctant blessing, she emigrated to the U.S. mainland and entered the graduate program at New York University.

▼▼▼▼▼▼

Nydia graduated from high school early. By the age of 16, she was already enrolled at the University of Puerto Rico in Rio Piedras.

Nydia Velázquez

In 1976 Nydia earned her master's degree in political science. She was offered a position as a political science instructor at the University of Puerto Rico and taught there until 1981, when the conservative New Progressive party came into power. Labeled a communist because she believed in workers' rights and social equality, she was harassed in Puerto Rico. She decided to return to New York, where she got a job teaching Puerto Rican studies at Hunter College of the City University of New York. In all, her teaching covered social science, political science, Puerto Rican government, and U.S. government.

Throughout her education and career, Nydia has done everything early. There was only one time when she felt uncomfortable pushing the age barrier. When she was 23, she became the chair of the Social Science department of the University of Puerto Rico, Humacao Campus. It was the only time, she says, when she felt a lot of pressure due to the attitudes of her fellow professors. "All of a sudden I found myself in a very awkward position because of the role reversal: Those who had been my professors—all of a sudden, I was their boss. I felt that as a newcomer, as a young person, and as a woman, I needed to prove myself to them. . . . It had to be the only time when I felt kind of uncomfortable, but I saw it as a challenge to prove myself. Because of a macho mentality of this culture—the Latino culture—the pressure was there."

NYDIA VELÁZQUEZ

Despite these challenges, Nydia was comfortable in her role and didn't imagine herself leaving the teaching profession. She had become a professor in order to teach others about politics but didn't think that she herself would ever run for political office. She says, "It never occurred to me while I was in college that I was getting a degree in political science because later on I would become politically active. Even my students in the classrooms at the University of Puerto Rico and later on at Hunter College were always telling me, 'You should run for political office,' and I'd say, 'No, no, no, that's not for me. That's not for me!'"

In 1983 Nydia got her first taste of activism in New York, followed shortly by her entry into politics. She got involved in politics because of one of her students. While a guest on a Spanish-language radio talk show discussing then-President Reagan's foreign policy toward the Caribbean, Nydia's voice was heard by a former student. He hadn't realized she was in New York, so he contacted the radio station and found her at Hunter College. The student invited Nydia to visit his family in Williamsburg, a section of Brooklyn. At that time, Nydia was living in Manhattan, and when she came to Williamsburg, an area of the city with a large Puerto Rican population, she says, "It was like a cultural shock, when I saw what I felt was the devastation of the community—buildings that were abandoned, garbage that wasn't collected.

▼▼▼▼▼

In 1983 Nydia got her first taste of political activism. She got involved in politics because of one of her students.

▲▲▲▲▲

NYDIA VELÁZQUEZ

Nydia asked Councilman Olmedo, "Why is it that the services provided in this community are not the same quality as what we see in Manhattan?"

And then I asked myself, 'Why? Why?' Up to that point I didn't have a real understanding or notion of what Puerto Ricans, the Puerto Rican community, were going through."

The student introduced Nydia to a Puerto Rican city councilman, Luis Olmedo. She asked Olmedo, "Why is it that the services provided here in this community are not the same quality as what we see in Manhattan?" He replied, "Well, because we don't have any political clout, any power." She asked, "What is it that the Puerto Rican community needs to do to achieve power?" and he said, "They're not registered to vote." Next she said, "In Puerto Rico, they vote! They have the highest percentage of political participation." He replied, "Well, here I think they don't trust the system, or there's the language barrier, and all that." To which she replied, "Well, I want to help. What is it that I need to do?" And he said, "Get a folding table and chairs and tell the people, 'See these cards? Just fill them out, and sign,' and that's it!" Nydia was amazed that giving people a voice could be so simple. The next Saturday she brought a folding table and two folding chairs and invited her students to help her register people to vote.

After she successfully registered a record number of Puerto Rican voters, she was chosen as Special Assistant to U.S. Representative Edolphus "Ed" Towns, a Democrat from Brooklyn. In this job, she dealt primarily with immigration issues and testified before Congress on immigration legislation.

A year later she became the first Latina appointed to serve on the New York City Council, filling a vacancy left by Luis Olmedo. From Hunter College, Nydia went to work for Towns, but, while she was working for him, Councilman Olmedo was convicted of federal conspiracy. Nydia says, "I was supported to fill the vacancy at that point, and I was appointed. I became the first Latina to serve on the City Council—not by election, but by appointment."

After her appointed term expired, she ran for the seat but was defeated. She learned a huge political lesson from this defeat: "I ran and I lost because I didn't have resources, I didn't have name recognition. But it was a great experience for me and I learned early on that you need to have a power base, that you need to develop a grassroots movement if you want to win. You cannot come in in a parachute and say, 'I'm here, I want to run for office.' You have to earn that."

After the council defeat, she was appointed by the governor of Puerto Rico to head the Migration Division Office of the Department of Labor and Human Resources in the United States. She remained at that post until 1989, when the governor of Puerto Rico, Rafael Hernandez Colon, named her to a cabinet-level position as Secretary of the Department of Puerto Rican Community Affairs, based in New York. "Because I had gotten so much involved in doing voter

▼▼▼▼▼

Nydia became the first Latina appointed to serve on the New York City Council.

▲▲▲▲▲▲

NYDIA VELÁZQUEZ

registration, the governor of Puerto Rico invited me to become the head of the office in the United States. And when I met with them, I said that the only way I can accept this is if you support my agenda of empowering Puerto Ricans politically in this country by promoting voter registration and voter participation. And he supported me, I accepted the job, and I launched one of the most successful voter registration drives of Puerto Ricans in the nation, called *Atrevete!* (Dare to Go for It!)"

As the Puerto Rican Community Affairs Secretary, Nydia ran the New York City headquarters and four regional offices. She advised the Puerto Rican government of the island's public policy and its commitment to Puerto Ricans on the U.S. mainland. When Hurricane Hugo ravaged Puerto Rico in 1989, Nydia personally contacted the head of the Joint Chiefs of Staff, General Colin Powell, and soon after that the island was promised federal assistance.

One of the community actions she is most proud of is *Atrevete!*, the Latino voter registration drive. This effort signed up 200,000 voters in the Northeast and Midwest. These new voters, many of them Puerto Rican, would help elect New York's first minority mayor, David Dinkins. In 1991 Nydia launched the project *Unidos Contra el SIDA* (United Against AIDS) to help fight the spread of AIDS among Hispanics.

Nydia Velázquez

New York's 12th District, which is 57 percent Hispanic, was created in 1992 to reflect a minority representation, in accordance with the National Voting Rights Act. When the 12th District was created, Nydia was one of three major Democratic candidates who ran in the primary; the other two were the conservative Elisabeth Colon and incumbent Congressman Stephan Solarz. Solarz was a well-known and leading member of Congress, but Nydia was supported by New York Mayor David Dinkins, Latino union leader Dennis Rivera, and African-American civil rights leader Jesse Jackson. She beat both Solarz and Colon, by 6 percentage points and 8 percentage points, respectively.

Winning the Democratic primary meant she was up against a Republican Hispanic, Angel Diaz, for the general election. She won easily, receiving 77 percent of the vote, while Diaz, a conservative, received only 20 percent.

Nydia was elected as the first Puerto Rican Congresswoman on November 5, 1992, representing New York's 12th District. Her district was one of nine new districts created that year to increase minority voting power under the National Voting Rights Act. The district includes a diverse ethnic mix, the neighborhoods of three boroughs, including Corona, Elmhurst, and Jackson Heights in Queens; the Lower East Side in Manhattan; and Williamsburg, Bushwick, Sunset Park, and East New York in Brooklyn. To Nydia, the biggest problem facing her district is

▼▼▼▼▼▼
Nydia was elected as the first Puerto Rican Congress-woman on November 5, 1992, representing New York's 12th District.
▲▲▲▲▲▲

Nydia Velázquez

Nydia addressed a news conference at her campaign headquarters on October 9, 1992.

"to empower this community not only politically but economically and culturally, in terms of education. For a community, this is one of the poorest districts in the nation," she explains. "As a person who grew up in poverty, I know what it takes to break away from poverty. To break the cycle of poverty, it takes educational

opportunity. And that's why education has been one of my biggest priorities in Congress. For poorer communities, the key to success is being able to provide the educational resources that these students need in order for them to learn and be able to compete."

After Nydia emerged the victor in the new district's primary, which virtually assured she would win the general election, she took a trip back to her hometown, accompanied by Mayor Dinkins and Dennis Rivera. Yabucoa rolled out the red carpet and embraced their heroine. Nydia thanked the crowd for its support and dedicated her victory to her mother and all the women of Puerto Rico. In an interview with *Newsday*, Yabucoa Mayor Angel Luis Ramos said of Nydia, "She represents a good example for the children. She came from a poor family and went to public school."

Nydia was sworn in as a Congresswoman by Judge Sonia (left). Her parents attended.

Nydia Velázquez

Nydia believes that she won because her Latino constituents knew of her and supported her. "At the time that this district was created, my name recognition citywide was extremely high—among Latinos," she explains. "But the status quo and the Anglo media, they didn't know that . . . and this is why we took them by surprise! All along, I had in my heart that I was the front-runner, and Steven Solarz knew this because he paid a lot of money for all the surveys that they conducted for him. In every survey that they ran, I was the front-runner. I was not a stranger coming here. I represented the district in the city council and then as the head of the Commonwealth of Puerto Rico; I was almost every single day in the media, in the Spanish media. But the mainstream media, they didn't know this. They didn't care. They didn't cover Latinos at that level, so I was someone new for them. But I wasn't new for my community."

Nydia understands well the needs of her constituents. Many of the people in her district are poor, many are immigrants, and a large group (22 percent) is on some form of public assistance. While most of the district is Hispanic (including not only Puerto Ricans, but also Dominicans, Colombians, and immigrants from other Spanish-speaking countries), there are also whites, African-Americans and Asian-Americans.

In 1994, Nydia was reelected to another two-year term as a U.S. Representative. To win a seat

Nydia Velázquez

in the 104th Congress, she had to beat out a fellow Hispanic Democrat in the primary, Pedro L. Velázquez (no relation). She got 82 percent of the vote to her opponent's 18 percent in the Democratic primary. Then, in the general election, she trounced the conservative candidate

The three Puerto Rican members of Congress: (from left to right) Luis Gutierrez (D–IL), Nydia Velázquez (D–NY), and José Serrano (D–NY).

In Congress, Nydia serves on the House Committee on Banking and Financial Services and on the Committee on Small Business.

▲▲▲▲▲▲

Nydia Velázquez

Genevieve R. Brennan, 92 percent to 6 percent. Since the Republicans had no candidate running for the seat, the victory was secure.

In Congress, Nydia serves on the House Committee on Banking and Financial Services (as a subcommittee member for Housing and Community Oversight and Housing and Community Opportunity) and on the Committee on Small Business (as a subcommittee member for Regulation and Paperwork). For Nydia, this committee work again means social responsibility. On the banking committee, for example, "We have to make sure that banks in our neighborhoods are operating, complying, with certain federal regulations. Banks coming into an area and opening up a branch have a moral and social responsibility to reinvest some of the profits that they make from our communities . . . into our communities," she explains.

Nydia was elected for her third term as New York Representative on November 5, 1996, serving in the 105th Congress. The constitutionality of race-based districts has been challenged, and in February 1997 a U.S. District Court ruled the 12th District unconstitutional on racial grounds. As of early 1997, the Supreme Court had not yet ruled whether the 12th District and others like it will fall as legal political divisions. In typical style, this doesn't bother Nydia. It's simply another challenge. "I don't think [the Supreme Court is] going to do anything until 1998," she says. "But we are getting ready and we will be ready. We are not going to just sit down and wait for them to rule. Even if they change my district, I'm going to get reelected. I'm going to win."

One of the causes that she has embraced is the freedom of Spanish-speakers to speak their native tongue and not be penalized. Those who believe that English should be the official language of government are known as supporters of English Only laws. Congresswoman Velázquez voiced her opposition to English Only laws by stating, "There are too many in America today, like proponents of English Only laws, who

Nydia (seated at far left) and First Lady Hillary Rodham Clinton (third from left) watch as a team of AmeriCorps volunteers mediate a mock debate for conflict resolution at Seward Park High School on the Lower East Side in Manhattan, New York.

seek to sow division rather than harmony. We must stand together and highlight the harsh impact the English Only movement will have on our language-minority constituents.

"We are all Americans and as such are all entitled to fair and equal access to the

Nydia shakes hands with revelers at the 1997 Puerto Rican Day Parade.

government," she declared. Fairness and equality are two things that Nydia has sought all her life. She has pledged to work for minorities in Congress and to improve the quality of life for people living in the nation's inner cities.

In her career she has moved back and forth between Puerto Rico and New York. More than once in her political campaigns her opponents have accused her of being too centered on Puerto Rico. However, the voters are resoundingly reelecting her, proving that the concerns she champions are not those of a narrow group but of the majority of her constituents.

Nydia Velázquez is clearly a woman of two worlds. She cherishes the world of her childhood, one of family unity and hard work. And while her roots are in a tropical land of palm trees, mangoes, and sugarcane fields, she has found purpose in a world of skyscrapers and subways. She also values the world of American politics, where she has learned that ordinary people can make a difference.

Nydia's advice for young people is to follow their dreams, no matter what. "The most important thing for any human being is to have faith in himself or herself. If you don't have faith in yourself, you cannot expect other people to believe that you can do it. And also, be determined. Whenever you want to do something, just focus on that and go for it! Don't let others change your mind, saying, 'No, you can't do this.'

"Whatever you want to become in life—Yes, you can do it—what it takes is determination and faith in yourself. Focus on the things you want to accomplish."

▼▼▼▼▼▼
Nydia values the world of American politics, where she has learned that ordinary people can make a difference.
▲▲▲▲▲▲

JIMMY SMITS

Actor
1955–

❝I think that what's important here is to reeducate the powers that be, and the public, that a Hispanic isn't necessarily one type of character or another. It's the same way as an actor's main job is to be versatile. I think he can be both versatile and Hispanic at the same time. **❞**

Jimmy Smits, as told to the *Chicago Tribune*

BIO HIGHLIGHTS

- Born July 9, 1955, in Brooklyn, New York; mother: Emelina, came from Puerto Rico; father: came from Suriname, in South America
- Attended public elementary school in Brooklyn, New York, and Thomas Jefferson High School in Brooklyn, graduating in 1972
- Earned B.A. degree from Brooklyn College, majoring in drama
- 1982, earned M.A. degree in theater from Cornell University
- Appeared in experimental version of *Hamlet* at New York's Joseph Papp Public Theater and in an off-Broadway play, *Buck*
- Got his first television acting job in the early 1980s in the daytime drama *All My Children*, playing a romantic leading man
- Made his film debut in *Running Scared* in 1986
- Won the 1987 Hispanic Media Image Task Force Imagen Award
- Nominated for an Emmy Award six consecutive times for his role as Victor Sifuentes on *L.A. Law*, in which he appeared from 1986 through 1991
- Won an Emmy Award for best actor in a dramatic series (*L.A. Law*) in 1990
- Appeared in several major films, including *Old Gringo*, *Switch*, and Oscar-nominated *My Family/Mi Familia*
- Received an Emmy for his portrayal of Detective Bobby Simone on *NYPD Blue*
- Nominated for an Independent Spirit Award for his role in *My Family/Mi Familia*, released in 1995
- 1996, won the Hispanic Heritage Award

Jimmy Smits

Jimmy Smits is known today as a handsome leading man, a successful actor, a devoted father, and a man committed to the advancement of the Hispanic community. Yet when he was a young boy growing up on the tough streets of Brooklyn, there were times when he felt like he didn't fit in.

Jimmy is also popularly known as one of the best-dressed men in show business. He looks like he stepped off the pages of *GQ* magazine. Yet when he was a child, Jimmy remembers having holes in his sneakers and wearing secondhand clothes.

What Jimmy says about his birth is: "I was over ten pounds—I was quite a large kid." Born into a devout Roman Catholic family, Jimmy, his two younger sisters, and his parents moved from borough to borough in New York City, then back to Puerto Rico, his mother's home, when Jimmy was 10. It was a culture shock for Jimmy. "It was one of the most traumatic things that ever happened to me," he said in a *Playboy* magazine interview. "I spoke no Spanish. But I had to go to school there. It really defined who I am. It formulated my cultural identity."

The family lived wherever Jimmy's father and mother could find jobs. They never went without food, shelter, or clothing—they were working-class people who had to make do with very little. Jimmy's father was in the merchant marines, then, later in life, became a factory manager in

New York. His mother worked as a nurse in Puerto Rico. Jimmy always made emotional adjustments to his new surroundings. To cope with his feelings he began to pretend—to act. "My childhood has a great deal to do with why I chose this profession [acting]," he told writer Gigi Anders. "You play by yourself a lot. You pretend. As dangerous and risky as it is, acting is very safe in the purest sense. It's not really you."

When Jimmy was 11, he and his family moved back to the United States from Puerto Rico for the last time, more or less settling in Brooklyn, New York. He told writer Tim Appelo, "I don't want to get my violin out, because it was a good thing, but trying to fit in with a new group, not having friends, just playing by yourself and making up things—that had a lot to do with planting the seeds of role-playing." In Jimmy's Brooklyn neighborhood, "There was high crime. There were drugs," he says. Jimmy has observed, "There are a lot of people I grew up with who aren't around anymore."

At Thomas Jefferson High School in Brooklyn, Jimmy played outside linebacker on the football team. But he also enjoyed being a star in the drama club. He couldn't be intensely involved in both. He said, "I found out I couldn't be in drama and football at the same time, so that was traumatic." But he says if he had stayed in football, "I would have had a twenty-inch neck."

▼▼▼▼▼▼

In Jimmy's Brooklyn neighborhood, there was a lot of crime. "There are a lot of people I grew up with who aren't around anymore."

▲▲▲▲▲▲

Jimmy Smits

▼▼▼▼▼▼

When Jimmy starred in a school play, the entire football team came to watch. Jimmy was worried that they had brought tomatoes to throw at him.

▲▲▲▲▲▲

When Jimmy starred in the school play, the whole football team came to watch his performance and sat in the front rows. They were a joke-playing, rowdy bunch, so Jimmy worried that they had brought tomatoes to throw at him. Instead, the audience rose in a standing ovation. About the football players, he remembers, "At the end, they all stood up and yelled, 'Yo, Jim!'"

Jimmy graduated from high school in 1972. He entered Brooklyn College as an education major. Although he became a father at the age of 19, when his daughter, Taina, was born, Jimmy stayed on his degree course. Jimmy's mother desperately wanted him to become a teacher, and Jimmy has always valued the importance of education. But the call to acting was just too strong. He earned his bachelor of arts degree in drama from Brooklyn College. Three years later he earned his master of fine arts degree in theater from Cornell University. He was the first in his family to get a college education.

His parents had emphasized, and he has always believed, that it is important for all children to get the best education they possibly can. In his talks to children, Jimmy stresses the importance of education. He promotes education as "the key to everything." As evidence of how important education is to him, in 1996 he volunteered his services for an attention-grabbing television spot on mentoring.

JIMMY SMITS

When he announced to his parents that he had chosen acting as his career, he says, his mother was upset at first. She had seen lots of out-of-work actors in New York City. She wanted him to do something more practical, something that would bring in a steady income. "She wasn't unsupportive, but she had come from a family of eleven, and my dad comes from a family of twelve. She thought this undertaking [acting] was unsecure. She was right," Jimmy says.

The talented young actor appeared in several critically acclaimed stage roles. Jimmy first found

Jimmy with long-time girlfriend, Wanda de Jesus

work in off-Broadway productions, and he appeared briefly as Horatio in the Joseph Papp Public Theater production of *Hamlet* under the direction of Joseph Papp. He was also seen in the Public Theater production of Michael Weller's *Ballad of Soapy Smith,* and he appeared in an off-Broadway show, *Buck,* with Morgan Freeman. He costarred off-Broadway with Linda Hunt in *Little Victories,* and in regional theater he appeared as a guest artist with the Colorado Shakespeare Festival and at the Center Stage in Baltimore.

Acting in live theater continues to be a passion for him. In Los Angeles in 1993, he appeared with his long-time girlfriend, Wanda de Jesus, in a three-month run

JIMMY SMITS

▼▼▼▼▼▼

Jimmy got his first break in television in the 1980s when he appeared on the daytime soap *All My Children.*

▲▲▲▲▲▲▲

of the intense drama *Death and the Maiden*, by Argentinean writer Ariel Dorfman. In college and in his early acting career, he concentrated on the classics. He believes that if an actor can master the language and demands of classical theater, then he can handle any role and bring depth to any character. In fact, Jimmy is open to anything that can increase his breadth as an actor (he even tried ballet during college).

Like many actors, Jimmy maintains homes in two cities. He needed the opportunities in film and television offered by both Hollywood and New York. To this day he divides his time between New York and Los Angeles, frequently flying to New York to see his children. Jimmy had moved out to California to test the waters, and in the mid-1980s he got his first break in television in the daytime drama *All My Children*, playing a romantic leading man. Later, he landed roles on *Another World, The Guiding Light*, and *One Life to Live.*

Jimmy and Wanda moved to Hollywood for good in 1995. With Wanda, an accomplished actress in her own right (*Santa Barbara, Live Shot*), he has a twelve-year relationship. The two of them "already feel married," she says, and they have what Jimmy calls "an ongoing discussion" about marriage and kids.

Jimmy's early work in soap operas set in motion his stature as a romantic leading man. The six-foot-three, brown-eyed, brown-haired actor is often cast as a love interest, but he is by no means limited to romantic roles. He has appeared as a comic lead, as a criminal, and as a historic figure. In the early years, he had to take roles that were not very good. He told a writer for the *Chicago Tribune*, "I've played everything from a Tibetan monk to some Banana Republic army captain." Some of those roles involved stereotypes, which Jimmy is intent on correcting. "The good news is that there are lots of roles out there for Hispanics. The bad news is that they are often as unshaven thugs," he told the *Chicago Tribune*.

After laboring in less-than-desirable roles, it was just a matter of time before his talent would land him on prime-time dramas. His first appearance was in 1984, when he was cast in the pilot episode of *Miami Vice* as Don Johnson's partner, who gets killed fifteen minutes into the show. He also appeared as a guest on the detective show *Spenser: For Hire*. But an even better role surfaced, that of lawyer Victor Sifuentes on the hit series *L.A. Law*. Jimmy auditioned badly for the role in New York, but he knew he was perfect for the part, so he flew to California and tried again. This time he got it.

It was a career-making role. As the Hispanic lawyer Victor Sifuentes, he was the voice of compassion in a world of sometimes-cutthroat lawyers. Jimmy told the *Chicago Tribune* why the part was so important to him: "I saw this as a chance to establish an intelligent, alternative

▼▼▼▼▼

In the early years, Jimmy had to accept roles that were not very good.

▲▲▲▲▲▲

Jimmy Smits

The cast of *L.A. Law.* From left to right: Richard Dysart, Corbin Bernsen, Michele Greene, Harry Hamlin, Susan Dey, Susan Ruttan, Alan Rachins, Jimmy Smits, and Michael Tucker (holding a balloon picture of Jill Eikenberry)

image [of Hispanics], someone who's neither a thug nor a womanizer." In 1990, after being nominated six times in six consecutive years, he won television's highest honor, an Emmy Award, for best actor in a dramatic series (*L.A. Law*). In 1988 the Hispanic Bar of Mexico honored him for improving the perception of Hispanic lawyers on *L.A. Law.*

After *L.A. Law*, Jimmy tried out other television staples: miniseries and made-for-TV

movies. In 1994 he played the lead in the Esparza-Katz production of *The Cisco Kid*, with Cheech Marín and Pedro Armendariz Jr. Jimmy's portrayal of the Cisco Kid (a Mexican adventurer

In 1987, *L.A. Law* was named Favorite New Dramatic Program at the People's Choice Awards.

who was popular on kids' television in the fifties) was mindful of Latino culture and not as comical as the original. Jimmy also appeared as Solomon in *Solomon and Sheba* on Showtime with Halle Berry in 1995. His other made-for-TV movies include *Glitz* (1988) and the ABC miniseries *The Tommyknockers* (1993), written by Stephen King.

Perhaps the greatest splash he has made as a television star and perhaps the most successful return anyone could make to television occurred in late 1994 when he joined the cast of *NYPD Blue*, a hit police drama (Jimmy had been offered the part when the series started, but he had turned it down to pursue movie roles). He

In *NYPD Blue*, Jimmy stars with Justine Miceli and Kim Delaney.

replaced David Caruso, who left after salary disputes with the network. At the time, the mainstream press was concerned if anyone could do a better job than the brooding Caruso, but

Smits more than rose to the occasion, proving his acting talents and audience appeal in the role of Detective Bobby Simone, drawing more fans to the show (the show rose from 29th to 8th in the Nielsen ratings during Jimmy's first season).

Bochco Productions' *NYPD Blue* has launched new standards for prime-time police dramas. Set against a vivid and volatile backdrop of the fascinating and sometimes seedy New York City, the policemen and women of the show push themselves to the limit—despite their personal problems—in doing their jobs and bringing criminals to justice. They are a group that is as dedicated to one another as they are to their jobs.

Once again Jimmy interpreted Hispanics in a positive light. Simone is, according to a network write-up, "a loner whose soft-spoken demeanor belies his complex personality and passionate spirit." He is in love with a beautiful yet troubled alcoholic, Detective Diane Russell, played by Kim Delaney. Simone is a strong, caring partner in their turbulent relationship, and he is also very supportive of his police partner, Detective Sipowicz, played by Dennis Franz.

Jimmy believes it is important that the show deals with real-life problems such as tension in relationships and personal choices that adults make in real life. He finds the theme of alcoholism fascinating: "The fact that [Diane] had an alcohol problem, and that the Sipowicz character, Dennis' character, is a recovering

▼▼▼▼▼▼

When Jimmy joined the cast of *NYPD Blue,* the show rose from 29th to 8th in the Nielsen ratings.

alcoholic—that's fertile ground for story lines. It's like a triangle thing, though not in the romantic sense." Some of the scenes and situations in this adult-themed drama involve nudity, but that is part of the show's realism. Jimmy explained to writer Gigi Anders, "This is a gritty show, an adult show, and sometimes—it's not every episode—there will be nudity."

In 1991, Jimmy appeared in the movie *Switch*.

Jimmy's career on the silver screen has covered a wide variety of roles. In his first starring role in a movie, he played a drug lord (*Running Scared*, a 1986 comedy with Billy Crystal), but the roles improved after that. He also starred as a police detective in a New York

JIMMY SMITS

City voodoo cult movie *The Believers* (1987, costarring Martin Sheen) and played revolutionary hero Pancho Villa in *Old Gringo* (1989). Next he was a surgeon instructor in *Vital Signs* (1990, a medical drama costarring Diane Lane and Adrian Pasdar). He also appeared in Gillian Armstrong's *Fires Within* (1991, a romance thriller costarring Greta Scacchi and Vincent D'Onofrio); Blake Edwards' *Switch* (1991, costarring Ellen Barkin, a comedy about changing genders), and the Hispanic epic *My Family/Mi Familia*.

Old Gringo, based on a book by Mexican writer Carlos Fuentes, provided an entrance to Hollywood for Spanish-language director Luis Puenzo. The production was beautifully filmed and told the story of a young revolutionary Mexican general Pancho Villa (played by Jimmy), a spinster (Jane Fonda), and the

In *Old Gringo*, Jimmy played Pancho Villa, a young revolutionary Mexican general.

elderly American writer Ambrose Bierce (Gregory Peck), set against the background of the Mexican Revolution. The film is a much more realistic view of Mexican history and the border area than most Hollywood movies, and Smits' Villa has been called the best portrayal of that historic figure in American film.

Jimmy became friends with veteran actor Gregory Peck while they were making *Old Gringo*. Smits hopes to grow old with his roles the same way Peck has. Jimmy calls Peck "la

JIMMY SMITS

crème de la crème . . . This man is Hollywood." He thinks that while it's important to play Hispanic roles and show a variety of images to the public, an actor shouldn't be limited to one type of role. "I think that what's important here is to reeducate the powers that be, and the public, that a Hispanic isn't necessarily one type of character or another. It's the same way as an actor's main job is to be versatile. I think he can be both versatile and Hispanic at the same time."

His strongest movie role so far has been in *My Family/Mi Familia,* an epic about several generations of a Mexican American family in California. It was coproduced by Anna Thomas and Francis Ford Coppola and written and directed by Gregory Nava (who also directed *El Norte*). This movie describes the experience of a certain group of Hispanic families in coming to the U.S., but it is also the story of all families. Critic Roger Ebert said of the movie, "Rarely have I felt at the movies such a sense of time and history, of stories and lessons passing down the generations, of a family living in its memories."

Jimmy attended a special screening of *My Family* in Washington, D.C., and afterward was invited to the White House to visit with President Bill Clinton. *My Family* had one of the most successful limited releases of 1995, and Jimmy's role as widower/ex-convict Jimmy Sanchez, described by *New York Times* critic Caryn James as "a terrific and dominant performance," added to the movie's success. It was nominated for an

▼▼▼▼▼▼

Jimmy thinks that while it's important to play Hispanic roles and show a variety of images to the public, an actor shouldn't be limited to one type of role.

▲▲▲▲▲▲

Oscar, and Jimmy was nominated for an Independent Spirit Award for his smoldering performance.

Jimmy has worked with writer/director Gregory Nava on several projects. Nava praises the actor's poise and professionalism. "I can't say enough about how talented this man is and what a beautiful person he is to work with," Nava told Josh Young of *Esquire*. He's a team player, and he gives all. Everybody in Hollywood is thinking about him now because of *NYPD Blue* and *My Family*."

In 1996 Jimmy hosted a series of television programs that appeared on networks across the country, particularly in areas with a high Hispanic population. The series, which is called *Hispanic Americans: The New Frontier*, was produced by Blue Pearl Entertainment, a Hispanic TV development company based in New York City. Each show addressed a particular portion of the Hispanic population: one was about the achievements of

In *My Family*, Jimmy played ex-convict Jimmy Sanchez. It was his most successful role to date.

JIMMY SMITS

Latinas, another about the achievements of entertainers. In the episode titled "Hispanics in the Media," Jimmy explained why it is so important for viewers to have true—rather than stereotyped—ideas about Hispanics in the public arena, such as newscasters, reporters, writers, and producers: "Whether it is film, print, radio, or television, we all have a bond with the media—it shapes and creates the perception and judgments that we have of ourselves . . . It entertains us and challenges us, and it takes us to places and events that are normally beyond our reach. It is the window to the world that we access daily. Many people think that there is a void in the way Hispanics are being represented."

Jimmy Smits is trying to fill that void in the best way he can—by playing in good roles as a consummate performer, and by giving back to his com-

Jimmy with Jennifer Lopez (who starred in *Selena*) at the National Council of La Raza Awards.

munity. The young boy from Brooklyn who learned early on that acting could put him in the shoes of others has grown into a man who is aware how important image is in the world. He is a willing and able representative of Hispanics, and he takes the cause of *la raza* to his heart. In 1991 he earned the tribute "King of Brooklyn," a title bestowed on ex-Brooklynites who come back to inspire and help their former neighbors.

Jimmy's dedication shows in the kinds of projects he takes on in his spare time. In 1996, Jimmy won a Hispanic Heritage Award, a special

The 1996 Hispanic Heritage Awards recipients attended a news conference in Washington. From left to right: Carmen Votaw, Jimmy Smits, Federico Peña, Isabel Allende, and Oscar de la Renta.

▼▼▼▼▼▼
Jimmy puts
his fame to
good use,
but
sometimes
he finds
stardom a
bit over-
whelming.
The lack of
privacy is
the only
negative he
finds in
acting.
▲▲▲▲▲▲

achievement for those Hispanics in the public eye who give back to their communities. These awards, given by Hispanics to Hispanics, are the highest honor one can get from one's own community. In early 1997, Jimmy got involved with a congressional task force headed by U.S. Representative Solomon Ortiz (D-Texas) to persuade Hollywood to give Hispanics more roles and more chances at front office and production jobs.

Jimmy clearly puts his fame to good use, but sometimes he finds stardom overwhelming. He told writer Tim Appelo that fame is a mixed blessing. "It has made me sad also, because of the privacy issue. My father is from Suriname and I went there with him three or four years ago, and nobody knew who I was, and it was great!"

Being a big star has its pressures. He is always under the microscope of public scrutiny. "I don't want people going through my closets and looking at how many pairs of sneakers I have. My feeling is, let the work speak for itself," he says. But the lack of privacy is the only negative Jimmy finds in acting. Otherwise, it's a career that has served him well, and he has brought dignity to acting in return.

INDEX

INDEX